SEAS

MW00831340

GRIEF
Finding Hope in Sorrow

Laura Kelly Fanucci

Little Rock
Scripture Study

A ministry of the Diocese of Little Rock
in partnership with Liturgical Press

Nihil obstat: Jerome Kodell, O.S.B., *Censor Librorum.*
Imprimatur: ✠ Anthony B. Taylor, Bishop of Little Rock, November 10, 2017.

Cover design by Ann Blattner. Cover photo: Getty Images. Used with permission.

Photos/illustrations: Pages 6, 9, 14, 16, 33, 35, 38, and 41, Getty Images. Used with permission. Page 12, *Naomi Entreating Ruth and Orpah to Return to the Land of Moab* by William Blake, 1795. Courtesy of Wikimedia Commons. Pages 19, 22, and 28, Goodsalt.com. Used with permission.

Scripture texts, prefaces, introductions, footnotes, and cross-references used in this work are taken from the *New American Bible, revised edition* © 2010, 1991, 1986, 1970 Confraternity of Christian Doctrine, Washington, DC and are used by permission of the copyright owner. All Rights Reserved. No part of the *New American Bible* may be reproduced in any form without permission in writing from the copyright owner.

ISBN: 978-0-8146-4503-1 (print); 978-0-8146-4528-4 (ebook)

Patricia Chiba 9/24/18
St. Mary's

Me Study

Contents

Introduction

Alive in the Word brings you resources to deepen your understanding of Scripture, offer meaning for your life today, and help you to pray and act in response to God's word.

Use any volume of **Alive in the Word** in the way best suited to you.

- **For individual learning and reflection,** consider this an invitation to prayerfully journal in response to the questions you find along the way. And be prepared to move from head to heart and then to action.
- **For group learning and reflection,** arrange for three sessions where you will use the material provided as the basis for faith sharing and prayer. You may ask group members to read each chapter in advance and come prepared with questions answered. In this kind of session, plan to be together for about an hour. Or, if your group prefers, read and respond to the questions together without advance preparation. With this approach, it's helpful to plan on spending more time for each group session in order to adequately work through each chapter.

- **For a parish-wide event** or use within a larger group, provide each person with a copy of this volume, and allow time during the event for quiet reading, group discussion and prayer, and then a final commitment by each person to some simple action in response to what he or she learned.

This volume on the topic of grief is one of several volumes that explore **Seasons of Our Lives**. While the Scriptures remain constant, we have the opportunity to find within them a fresh message as we go through life facing various challenges. Whether the circumstances in our lives change due to our own decisions or due to the natural process of aging and maturing, we bring with us the actual lived experiences of this world to our prayerful reading of the Bible. This series provides an opportunity to acknowledge our own circumstances and to find how God continues to work in us through changing times.

Our Grief

Begin by asking God to be with you in your prayer and study. Then read through Ruth 1:1-18, the beginning of a story of survival through grief.

Ruth 1:1-18

[1]Once back in the time of the judges there was a famine in the land; so a man from Bethlehem of Judah left home with his wife and two sons to reside on the plateau of Moab. [2]The man was named Elimelech, his wife Naomi, and his sons Mahlon and Chilion; they were Ephrathites from Bethlehem of Judah. Some time after their arrival on the plateau of Moab, [3]Elimelech, the husband of Naomi, died, and she was left with her two sons. [4]They married Moabite women, one named Orpah, the other Ruth. When they had lived there about ten years, [5]both Mahlon and Chilion died also, and the woman was left with neither her two boys nor her husband.

[6]She and her daughters-in-law then prepared to go back from the plateau of Moab because word had reached her there

that the LORD had seen to his people's needs and given them food. ⁷She and her two daughters-in-law left the place where they had been living. On the road back to the land of Judah, ⁸Naomi said to her daughters-in-law, "Go back, each of you to your mother's house. May the LORD show you the same kindness as you have shown to the deceased and to me. ⁹May the LORD guide each of you to find a husband and a home in which you will be at rest." She kissed them good-bye, but they wept aloud, ¹⁰crying, "No! We will go back with you, to your people." ¹¹Naomi replied, "Go back, my daughters. Why come with me? Have I other sons in my womb who could become your husbands? ¹²Go, my daughters, for I am too old to marry again. Even if I had any such hope, or if tonight I had a husband and were to bear sons, ¹³would you wait for them and deprive yourselves of husbands until those sons grew up? No, my daughters, my lot is too bitter for you, because the LORD has extended his hand against me." ¹⁴Again they wept aloud; then Orpah kissed her mother-in-law good-bye, but Ruth clung to her.

¹⁵"See now," she said, "your sister-in-law has gone back to her people and her god. Go back after your sister-in-law!" ¹⁶But Ruth said, "Do not press me to go back and abandon you!

> Wherever you go I will go,
>   wherever you lodge I will lodge.
> Your people shall be my people
>   and your God, my God.
> ¹⁷Where you die I will die,
>   and there be buried.

May the LORD do thus to me, and more, if even death separates me from you!" [18]Naomi then ceased to urge her, for she saw she was determined to go with her.

After a few moments of quiet reflection on the passage, consider the information provided in Setting the Scene.

Setting the Scene

Grief is universal. The Old Testament overflows with stories of sorrow. Job lost everything and struggled with faith in the face of despair. The book of Lamentations sings a lament of communal suffering. The Psalms give voice to the sadness, anger, and fear of people overwhelmed by death, disease, and desolation. But the book of Ruth offers a unique glimpse into the dynamics of grief. As the story of two women bound together by shared devastation, this book portrays the full range of human responses to suffering and death. We see Naomi and Ruth experience despair, anger, depression, confusion, and sadness—but also compassion, comfort, determination, and hope. The book stands as a testimony to the power of love and the strength of human resilience. Ruth is a story of our grief: the emotions, experiences, and even unexpected new beginnings that arise from significant suffering.

Grief can spring from a variety of loves and losses, many of which are reflected in Ruth and Naomi's story. Grief can come from the death of a parent, spouse, child, sibling, grandparent, relative, or friend. Grief can emerge from secondary losses like the loss of a homeland, job, or relationship. Grief can spring from silent sufferings like infertility, miscarriage, addiction, infidelity, or divorce. As Naomi and Ruth make their way through shock and sorrow following the deaths of their beloveds, the two women ultimately forge a new future together that grounds their shared faith in a firm and unshakable foundation. Turning to their story when we are suffering can open our eyes to the empathy and companionship that Scripture offers us as we grieve.

The entire passage will be considered a few verses at a time. The questions in the margins are for discussion with others. If you are using these materials on your own, use the questions for personal reflection or as a guide to journaling.

Understanding the Scene Itself

¹Once back in the time of the judges there was a famine in the land; so a man from Bethlehem of Judah left home with his wife and two sons to reside on the plateau of Moab. ²The man was named Elimelech, his wife Naomi, and his sons Mahlon and Chilion; they were Ephrathites from

Bethlehem of Judah. Some time after their arrival on the plateau of Moab, ³Elimelech, the husband of Naomi, died, and she was left with her two sons. ⁴They married Moabite women, one named Orpah, the other Ruth. When they had lived there about ten years, ⁵both Mahlon and Chilion died also, and the woman was left with neither her two boys nor her husband.

Suffering starts from the first sentence of the book of Ruth. As we are introduced to Elimelech's family, we hear of famine, hunger, and the loss of homeland. Moving to Moab would have been no small feat for a family from Judah, since the Israelites' stance toward these foreigners was harsh: "No Ammonite or Moabite may ever come into the assembly of the LORD, nor may any of their descendants even to the tenth generation come into the assembly of the LORD, because they would not come to meet you with food and water on your journey after you left Egypt" (Deut 23:4-5). Yet as often happens, the reality of need and desperation drives people to leave their home.

The family settles into a strange land, but soon tragedy strikes with Elimelech's death. After their father dies, Mahlon and Chilion marry Moabite women in direct violation of the Mosaic law (Ezra 9:1-2; Neh 13:23-27). Yet presumably the situation is acceptable to their families as Orpah and Ruth develop a warm and caring relationship with their mother-in-law, seen later in the story. However, the meaning of the sons' names—derived from "weakness" and "consumption"—indicate a sense of foreboding and may suggest poor health as the cause of their untimely deaths. Sure enough, a decade later both men die, leaving Naomi bereft.

From the opening lines of this story, Naomi's losses pile up and overwhelm her: first her husband and then both her sons are gone. The end of verse 5 speaks of Naomi's devastation in simple, stark terms. Much like Job, who lost his children, property, and health, Naomi has lost everything. The death of her husband and sons meant not only the loss of family and companionship but also financial security, personal protection, and social identity. Without men, women in this society held no significance. Ruth and Orpah are equally bereft without their husbands. No children are mentioned for either one, suggesting that childlessness might have been an additional sorrow and burden, as women were defined by their roles as wives and mothers. All three would have been doomed to a life of poverty, prostitution, or starvation if they could not remarry or return to their family's home. Death has a powerful ripple effect, upending every aspect of life into uncertainty.

> Have you ever felt overwhelmed by loss like Naomi? Where did you turn to find comfort?

> What have been "secondary losses" you have experienced from the death of a loved one, like the loss of other relationships, common interests, or a sense of home? How have you dealt with these unexpected parts of grief?

⁶She and her daughters-in-law then prepared to go back from the plateau of Moab because word had reached her there that the LORD had seen to his people's needs and given them food. ⁷She and her two daughters-in-law left the place where they had been living. On the road back to the land of Judah, ⁸Naomi said to her daughters-in-law, "Go back, each of you to your mother's

house. May the LORD show you the same kindness as you have shown to the deceased and to me. ⁹May the LORD guide each of you to find a husband and a home in which you will be at rest." She kissed them good-bye, but they wept aloud, ¹⁰crying, "No! We will go back with you, to your people." ¹¹Naomi replied, "Go back, my daughters. Why come with me? Have I other sons in my womb who could become your husbands? ¹²Go, my daughters, for I am too old to marry again. Even if I had any such hope, or if tonight I had a husband and were to bear sons, ¹³would you wait for them and deprive yourselves of husbands until those sons grew up? No, my daughters, my lot is too bitter for you, because the LORD has extended his hand against me."

In verse 6, Naomi decides to return home to Judah in search of food. Now it is Ruth and Orpah's turn to face the loss of their own homeland, while Naomi again prepares to leave behind a country she has come to know. This decision must have weighed heavily on all three women, reflecting how we are often forced to make life-changing decisions in the immediate aftermath of a loved one's death. The complicated nature of Naomi's faith after grief is revealed in this passage. Verse 6 shows her to be a woman of faith despite her suffering, desiring to follow where God is working. In verses 8-9, she asks God's blessings upon her daughters-in-law. Yet her words in verse 13 make clear that she feels God has turned against her. Naomi's reactions illustrate how grief can lead us to experience multiple emotions or conflicting beliefs simultaneously.

When have you felt conflicted in grief or experienced different emotions at once?

Naomi claims the lion's share of the grief, having lost her husband and sons. Unlike her daughters-in-law, she is too old to remarry, so she laments that she can replace nothing she has lost. Later in the chapter, Naomi declares that she wants a new name, proof of how she now feels defined by grief and resentment: "Do not call me Naomi ['Sweet']. Call me Mara ['Bitter'], for the Almighty has made my life very bitter. I went away full, but the LORD has brought me back empty. Why should you call me 'Sweet,' since the LORD has brought me to trial, and the Almighty has pronounced evil sentence on me" (vv. 20-21). Naomi cannot see beyond her grief and now views the world as a conflict between her and God. Her honesty shows how loss can change our whole worldview as it redefines relationships, beliefs, identities, and our sense of belonging.

The author of Ruth does not begrudge Naomi's bitterness or judge her anger. Our hearts ache for Naomi, for she believes God's hand has turned against her. Her words bear a striking resemblance to Job's: "He has cast me into the mire; / I have become like dust and ashes. / I cry to you, but you do not answer me; / I stand, but you take no notice. / You have turned into my tormentor, / and with your strong

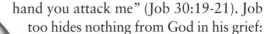

hand you attack me" (Job 30:19-21). Job too hides nothing from God in his grief: "My own utterance I will not restrain; / I will speak in the anguish of my spirit; / I will complain in the bitterness of my soul" (Job 7:11). Naomi's lament also captures the anguish of the psalmist, who does not soften any hard edge of his grief to make it more palatable: "Your arrows have sunk deep in me; / your hand has come down upon me" (Ps 38:3). Anger at God is a natural reaction when faced with crippling loss, but its presence within Scripture reminds us that lament is still sacred prayer. Many psalms give voice to grief (see Pss 13; 22; 69; and 88). As a woman of faith, Naomi would have had the words of the psalms on her lips and heart. We too can find solidarity in their cries from the pit of darkness.

Have you been able to bring your honest emotions to God in prayer? What might happen if you shared with God the depths of your sorrow, fear, or anger?

The three women leave Moab together, but then Naomi changes her mind, declaring that her daughters-in-law should return to their homes in Moab. Perhaps she is pushing them away out of sorrow or perhaps she reconsiders that it would be better for Ruth and Orpah to remain with their people. Whatever her rationale, she blesses her daughters-in-law with words of gratitude for their compassion and hope for a brighter future. The touching description of their kisses and weeping shows the genuine affection between the women (v. 9). But Orpah and Ruth reveal their own strength, protesting Naomi's decision (v. 10). They speak in unison, showing a united front of loyalty to their mother-in-law and concern for her suffering. Yet Naomi persists in what she feels is best in the worst of situations. She calls them "daughters" out of love, yet insists they turn back, saying "go" three times.

¹⁴Again they wept aloud; then Orpah kissed her mother-in-law good-bye, but Ruth clung to her.
¹⁵"See now," she said, "your sister-in-law has gone back to her people and her god. Go back after your sister-in-law!" ¹⁶But Ruth said, "Do not press me to go back and abandon you!

Wherever you go I will go,
    wherever you lodge I will lodge.
Your people shall be my people
    and your God, my God.
¹⁷Where you die I will die,
    and there be buried.

May the LORD do thus to me, and more, if even death separates me from you!" ¹⁸Naomi then ceased to urge her, for she saw she was determined to go with her.

Here lies the emotional climax of the book of Ruth. Verse 14 draws us into the intimacy of the women's affection: weeping, kissing farewell, and clinging together. Orpah decides to leave, perhaps out of loving obedience to her mother-in-law's wishes. Her decision demonstrates how people make different decisions in grief; there is not one single right way to respond to the events

Have you ever wrestled with decisions that others have made while grieving? How have friends or family struggled to understand your own grief?

or emotions that arise after loss. Again the author passes no judgment on any of the women, inviting us to see the range of their responses as faithful and compassionate.

In verse 16, Ruth speaks for herself for the first time. She is bold and strong, making a loving declaration of fidelity and faith. She promises to stay with Naomi no matter what happens, making this vow before God in the tradition of formal oaths of loyalty (as in 1 Sam 20:13-17). Ruth decrees that her entire identity will be defined by Naomi, her people, and her God. She will stay with her even to death and be buried near her—a powerful statement for two women so closely acquainted with death. Ruth pledges the whole of her life in love. She too is transformed by grief, but for good. Ruth's words are among the most moving and beautiful in the entire Bible.

Who has stayed by your side through your grieving? Have you felt God present with you in times of struggle?

Naomi sees the depth of Ruth's resolve and accepts her companionship (v. 18). The two women begin to make their journey together into a new chapter of life. The final message of this passage is clear: clinging together is what

carries us through grief—back to God and forward into new life. Ruth and Naomi offer a powerful example of how to unite within devastating circumstances across age, race, background, or temperament. While loss is universal, so is the invitation to grow through grief and to help each other remember we are never alone.

Praying the Word / Sacred Reading

Return to the passage in Ruth 1, reading it slowly and prayerfully. What words or phrases speak to you? Let yourself linger with these words or phrases as you let God speak to you.

As you return to the passage, notice what word or phrase grabs your attention. Perhaps this word or phrase leads you toward either Ruth or Naomi in your prayer. At times some of us feel like Naomi in our grief: overwhelmed, angry, bitter, or despairing. At times we can feel like Ruth: strong, loving, faithful, or hopeful. Many times we may feel like a mixture of both. When have you felt like Naomi? When have you felt like Ruth?

Imagine what God might be inviting you to consider as you reflect on each woman's emotions and experience. How might she become a companion for you as you move forward into a new chapter in life after loss?

Living the Word

Grief changes over time. It is rarely linear, but cycles through ups and downs. By the end of the book, Ruth remarries and has a son with her new husband Boaz, making her the great-grandmother of David. Naomi's joy at her unexpected blessing—her own rebirth as grandmother—reveals how Scripture's story of salvation itself winds through times of deep grief. While grief never ends completely, it can evolve as it leads us into new life beyond sorrow. This week let yourself imagine—even for a brief moment—what it might be like to feel joy and happiness again. Can you trust that grief and loss are not the end of your story, but that new companions, callings, or opportunities for growth might eventually emerge? Ask God for the strength to hope and the courage to believe in light even within present darkness.

God's Grief

Begin by asking God to guide you in your prayer and study. Then read through a portion of John 11, a story of Jesus' own grief.

John 11:1-7, 17-27, 32-44

¹Now a man was ill, Lazarus from Bethany, the village of Mary and her sister Martha. ²Mary was the one who had anointed the Lord with perfumed oil and dried his feet with her hair; it was her brother Lazarus who was ill. ³So the sisters sent word to him, saying, "Master, the one you love is ill." ⁴When Jesus heard this he said, "This illness is not to end in death, but is for the glory of God, that the Son of God may be glorified through it." ⁵Now Jesus loved Martha and her sister and Lazarus. ⁶So when He heard that He was ill, He remained for two days in the place where he was. ⁷Then after this he said to his disciples, "Let us go back to Judea."

¹⁷When Jesus arrived, he found that Lazarus had already been in the tomb for four days. ¹⁸Now Bethany was near Jerusalem, only about two miles away. ¹⁹And many of the Jews had come to Martha and Mary to comfort them about their brother. ²⁰When Martha heard that Jesus was coming, she went to meet him; but Mary sat at home. ²¹Martha said to Jesus, "Lord, if you had been here, my brother would not have died. ²²[But] even now I know that whatever you ask of God, God will give you." ²³Jesus said to her, "Your brother will rise." ²⁴Martha said to him, "I know he will rise, in the resurrection on the last day." ²⁵Jesus told her, "I am the resurrection and the life; whoever believes in me, even if he dies, will live, ²⁶and everyone who lives and believes in me will never die. Do you believe this?" ²⁷She said to him, "Yes, Lord. I have come to believe that you are the Messiah, the Son of God, the one who is coming into the world."

³²When Mary came to where Jesus was and saw him, she fell at his feet and said to him, "Lord, if you had been here, my brother would not have died." ³³When Jesus saw her weeping and the Jews who had come with her weeping, he became perturbed and deeply troubled, ³⁴and said, "Where have you laid him?" They said to him, "Sir, come and see." ³⁵And Jesus wept. ³⁶So the Jews said, "See how he loved him." ³⁷But some of them said, "Could not the one who opened the eyes of the blind man have done something so that this man would not have died?"

³⁸So Jesus, perturbed again, came to the tomb. It was a cave, and a stone lay across it. ³⁹Jesus

said, "Take away the stone." Martha, the dead man's sister, said to him, "Lord, by now there will be a stench; he has been dead for four days." [40]Jesus said to her, "Did I not tell you that if you believe you will see the glory of God?" [41]So they took away the stone. And Jesus raised his eyes and said, "Father, I thank you for hearing me. [42]I know that you always hear me; but because of the crowd here I have said this, that they may believe that you sent me." [43]And when He had said this, He cried out in a loud voice, "Lazarus, come out!" [44]The dead man came out, tied hand and foot with burial bands, and his face was wrapped in a cloth. So Jesus said to them, "Untie him and let him go."

After a few moments of quiet reflection on the passage, consider the information provided in Setting the Scene.

Setting the Scene

"Jesus wept" (John 11:35). This powerful, compact sentence—commonly known as the shortest Bible verse because of its brevity in certain translations—speaks volumes. The brief statement of emotion distills the heart of God into two short words, much like the name of God given in Exodus: "I am" (Exod 3:14). The juxtaposition of these two phrases draws a tight-knit unity between living and suffering: to be is to grieve. Jesus' sorrow at Lazarus' death reveals that grief is part of who God is and what God does. God's grief comes from being in relationship with humanity, loving people, and desiring good for them. Throughout Scripture, the sight of human suffering causes God to weep, and few things are more comforting in grief than to remember we are seen by a God who mourns with us.

Lazarus' death and raising is a story of lament and love, drawn from what is called the "Book of Signs" in the Gospel of John (1:19–12:50). Scholars identify seven signs or wondrous acts of Jesus in this gospel: turning water into wine, curing the royal official's son in Capernaum, healing the paralyzed man at Bethesda, feeding the five thousand, walking on water, healing the man born blind, and raising Lazarus. The number seven in Scripture symbolizes wholeness, and these seven signs give us a complete picture of who Jesus is—with triumph over death as the ultimate sign, prefiguring Jesus' own resurrection. The raising of Lazarus is also a sign for those of us who are mourning, that death and sorrow are not the end of the story. The incarnation (God made flesh) and the resurrection (God triumphing over death) fold together in this passage. Jesus is the mourner and the savior. As he stands by the tomb and weeps, as so many of us have done, he reminds us again what the fullness of his humanity means: there is nowhere we can go where he has not already been.

He will never leave

The entire passage will be considered a few verses at a time. The questions in the margins (as above) are for discussion with others. If you are using these materials on your own, use the questions for personal reflection or as a guide to journaling.

Understanding the Scene Itself

¹Now a man was ill, Lazarus from Bethany, the village of Mary and her sister Martha. ²Mary was the one who had anointed the Lord with perfumed oil and dried his feet with her hair; it was her brother Lazarus who was ill. ³So the sisters sent word to him, saying, "Master, the one you love is ill." ⁴When Jesus heard this He said, "This illness is not to end in death, but is for the glory of God, that the Son of God may be glorified through it." ⁵Now Jesus loved Martha and her sister and Lazarus. ⁶So when He heard that he was ill, He remained for two days in the place where he was. ⁷Then after this he said to his disciples, "Let us go back to Judea."

The opening of this story—a loved one becoming sick—is the beginning of many of our experiences of grief. The first sentences of John 11 give us the setting and characters of the story, although interestingly one of the three siblings is identified by an encounter that does not happen until the next chapter of John, when Mary anoints Jesus' feet (12:1-8). Clearly the story would have been well known, and the names of Lazarus, Mary, and Martha immediately recognized by early Christians. Furthermore, the name

Lazarus (meaning "God has helped") would have hinted at how the story might unfold. Jesus' response to the news of his friend's illness in verse 4 is not as callous or dismissive as it may first seem on the surface. Instead, for the same reason that Jesus gave sight to the man born blind ("so that the works of God might be made visible through him" [9:3]), he will bring glory to God from Lazarus' illness. While Jesus did not prevent the suffering from happening, He can still bring forth goodness.

Verse 5 is a powerful statement of Jesus' love for his friends. Besides the beloved disciple, the only individuals specifically named by John as being loved by Jesus are Martha, Mary, and Lazarus. Yet even though verses 6-7 seem strange in light of this love, the reasons for Jesus' delay will soon be revealed. Love is linked to death throughout the Gospel of John (3:16; 15:13), and even Jesus' closest friends are not spared deepest suffering. Jesus himself will be led by love back to Bethany, at the heart of Judea where the dangerous opposition against him is mounting.

¹⁷**When Jesus arrived, he found that Lazarus had already been in the tomb for four days. ¹⁸Now Bethany was near Jerusalem, only about two miles away. ¹⁹And many of the Jews had come to Martha and Mary to comfort them about their brother. ²⁰When Martha heard that Jesus was coming, she went to meet him; but Mary sat at home. ²¹Martha said to Jesus, "Lord, if you had been here, my brother would not have died. ²²[But] even now I know that whatever you**

When have you experienced illness (your own or others') as a catalyst for God's work in your life?

When have you felt that God delayed in coming to you or answering your prayer?

In many occasions because God will answer

ask of God, God will give you." [23]Jesus said to her, "Your brother will rise." [24]Martha said to him, "I know he will rise, in the resurrection on the last day." [25]Jesus told her, "I am the resurrection and the life; whoever believes in me, even if he dies, will live, [26]and everyone who lives and believes in me will never die. Do you believe this?" [27]She said to him, "Yes, Lord. I have come to believe that you are the Messiah, the Son of God, the one who is coming into the world."

The significance of Lazarus being in the tomb for four days relates to Jewish traditions surrounding death (v. 17). First-century Jews believed that the soul lingered with the deceased for three days, hoping the body might come back to life. So, after four days, it would be certain that the spirit of Lazarus would be gone and his body beginning to decay. Jesus intentionally delayed his arrival so that He would be dealing with the reality (even the stench) of death. Jewish mourning rituals are already underway, as people have gathered at the home of Mary and Martha to comfort them. Yet Martha leaves home and goes out to meet Jesus before He arrives in Bethany, already revealing the strength and determination of her faith. She is unafraid to confront Jesus directly. Her trust in him makes her certain that his presence could have stopped her brother's death (v. 21). Yet she does not remain stuck in resentment. She reaffirms her belief that Jesus could still intervene on her behalf to God, a powerful testimony in the face of death.

If you could speak to Jesus directly and honestly about your grief, what would you say?

> **Jesus transforms an abstract belief into a startlingly concrete reality: the resurrection is not a far-off event but the friend standing with Martha.**

When Jesus plainly tells Martha that her brother will rise, she responds with immediate acceptance, echoing traditional Jewish beliefs in a communal resurrection of the faithful at the end of time. But Jesus pushes the meaning of her own words by identifying himself as the resurrection and the life (v. 25). This is one of seven "I am" statements in the Gospel of John, which are central to the gospel writer's theological understanding of Jesus. Here Jesus transforms an abstract belief into a startlingly concrete reality: the resurrection is not a far-off event but the friend standing before Martha. This promise is a person. Martha's statement of faith in verse 27 becomes even more stunning when we consider how Jesus' statement might have shocked someone who thought she knew him well. Yet Martha stands unwavering in her belief, affirming Jesus as the Messiah and the Son of God—two titles that have never before been put together in John's gospel. She also identifies Jesus as "coming into the world," signaling that his work is already ongoing but not yet complete—just as his action in this story has only begun.

What do Jesus' words—"I am the resurrection and the life"—mean for your own faith? Do you find his words comforting or challenging?

³²When Mary came to where Jesus was and saw him, she fell at his feet and said to him, "Lord, if you had been here, my brother would not have died." ³³When Jesus saw her weeping and the Jews who had come with her weeping, he became perturbed and deeply troubled, ³⁴and said, "Where have you laid him?" They said to him, "Sir, come and see." ³⁵And Jesus wept. ³⁶So the Jews said, "See how he loved him." ³⁷But some of them said, "Could not the one who opened the eyes of the blind man have done something so that this man would not have died?"

In contrast with her sister's theological discussion, Mary's encounter with Jesus is intensely emotional. She falls at his feet and weeps. Like Martha, she is unafraid to directly confront Jesus with her pain and longing, using the same words that her sister spoke on behalf of their brother (v. 32). Mary models bold faith, willing to bring her deepest desires and sorrow to Jesus. Perhaps she is struggling more with Lazarus' death (suggesting why Martha went out to Jesus first while Mary stayed back with the mourners), or perhaps she expresses emotions more intensely than her sister. Grief is always personal, and here again the portrayal of bereavement offers multiple portraits of people's responses to death. Likewise, the range of the Jews' reactions (vv. 36-37) illustrates how grief can lead people to

Who has wept with you in your sorrow? How has the presence of others (like the Jews who came to weep with Mary and Martha) affected your grief?

notice signs of God's love or to rage with accusation, doubting God's nature as good or powerful.

Verse 33 offers a remarkable insight into Jesus' humanity and divinity. A close reading reveals that it is not the fact of Lazarus' death (which Jesus learned about in verse 17) but the sight of others' weeping that causes Jesus to grieve. Human suffering and the love of the living for the dead are what move God to tears. Jesus knows the depths of human emotion, like the Suffering Servant in Isaiah: "a man of suffering, knowing pain" (Isa 53:3). He is fully human, both physically (crying real tears) and emotionally (mourning a beloved friend). He is also fully divine: weeping for all of humanity, weeping at the heartbreak of death, and weeping with all who mourn. What is translated in verse 33 as "perturbed" is a Greek phrase referring to snorting in anger like a horse. Other translations say Jesus was "greatly disturbed in spirit" or "deeply moved and troubled." Unlike the calm,

unruffled Jesus who delayed two days before coming to Bethany, this Jesus is now deeply unsettled. Even though as God he knows death is not final, he is still full of sorrow and empathy for his people.

The Psalms often remind us that God sees our grief: "Why should the wicked scorn God, / say in their hearts, 'God does not care'? / But you do see; / you take note of misery and sorrow; / you take the matter in hand"

(Ps 10:13-14). The power of sight in the story of Lazarus continues with the Jews' invitation to Jesus to "come and see" (v. 35). Jesus still has not seen the tomb or body of his friend (as he does not arrive at the tomb until later, verse 38). But the people's plea to come and see is the catalyst for his tears—an invitation that echoes the words of Jesus' call to the disciples in John 1:39. The tables have turned as the people call out now to Jesus, reminding us that we have an impact on God in our relationship, too.

What does it mean to you that God weeps for and with us?

³⁸So Jesus, perturbed again, came to the tomb. It was a cave, and a stone lay across it. ³⁹Jesus said, "Take away the stone." Martha, the dead man's sister, said to him, "Lord, by now there will be a stench; he has been dead for four days." ⁴⁰Jesus said to her, "Did I not tell you that if you believe you will see the glory of God?" ⁴¹So they took away the stone. And Jesus raised his eyes and said, "Father, I thank you for hearing me. ⁴²I know that you always hear me; but because of the crowd here I have said this, that they may believe that you sent me." ⁴³And when he had said this, he cried out in a loud voice, "Lazarus, come out!" ⁴⁴The dead man came out, tied hand and foot with burial bands, and his face was wrapped in a cloth. So Jesus said to them, "Untie him and let him go."

Again greatly disturbed, Jesus finally comes to the tomb. He orders the same action that will happen at his own resurrection—the stone to be rolled away. Jesus calls upon the people to get

What new opportunity or growth might God be calling you to, from your grief?

God's Grief 29

God wants us to be active partners in bringing new life after death.

involved as part of this miracle (the same reason he will ask them to untie Lazarus' burial bands in verse 44). This act reminds us that we have a role to play in God's work—an important invitation to remember when we feel like victims in grief, unable to control events or emotions. God still wants us to be active partners in bringing forth new life after death.

Two more details in this passage speak to us in grief. First, when Jesus looks up to heaven and prays for God's intercession—the first time he speaks directly to God in John's gospel—he addresses God as Father. This intimate term encourages us to see God as a caring parent who rushes to console a weeping child. Second, Jesus thanks God for hearing him, and then Lazarus is raised when he hears Jesus' voice. Jesus shows that his sheep do recognize the voice of the shepherd (10:3), and that the voice of God will lead us from death into life (5:28). The "glory of God" (vv. 4 and 40) is tied to this relationship of call and response: we can call upon God and be heard, and when we act upon hearing God's voice, new life can come from death.

Have you experienced God's comfort through something you heard— someone's words, a moving song, or a prayer?

Ironically, Jesus' resurrection of Lazarus puts his own death into motion (12:1-11), yet God cannot help but intervene where people are suffering. The ultimate result of Lazarus' raising is release: he is unbound. But Jesus does not embrace

Lazarus, nor do his sisters rush to him rejoicing. Lazarus himself never speaks, and we hear little about his life after being raised—only that he joins Jesus at table (12:1-2) and becomes a target of the chief priests' hatred (12:10-11). The focus of the gospel's author seems to be what comes before the miracle. The bereaved, not the dead, have taken precedence in Jesus' care and concern. So we, too, can trust that our own weeping and sadness are seen and known by our loving God.

Praying the Word / Sacred Reading

Return to the passage in John 11, reading it slowly and prayerfully. Now imagine yourself into the scene as you ask God to open your heart to new perspectives on the story.

If you are using this study with a group, allow for time to read the full passage silently. Then you may wish to have one person read the reflection below while the others consider the questions quietly.

The power of John 11:35—"And Jesus wept"—can become a simple refrain to carry into prayer. As you move into your work and activities this week, keep this verse in mind. You might even want to write it on a piece of paper to keep in your pocket.

See what happens when you add the words "and Jesus wept" to your own thoughts, especially when you are struggling with grief or sorrow. Notice how it feels to pray the refrain as you hear others' stories of suffering or read difficult stories in the news. As you imagine Jesus weeping with you or with others, how does your perspective on sorrow and grief change? Can you draw comfort or consolation if you imagine Jesus weeping today?

Living the Word

At first glance, the end of Lazarus' story may feel frustrating for us. Our loved one was not brought back from the dead, no matter how much we prayed or pleaded with God. We wanted this miracle, the magical fix for our mourning. But what we are given instead is the deeper message of the story: that our God is a God of compassion who weeps with us. What a gift to have a God who is greatly disturbed and deeply moved—not an unmoved mover or a distant stoic. Jesus has stood weeping at his friend's grave, so he can fully share in our sorrow.

The Catholic devotion to the Sacred Heart of Jesus speaks to the compassion we find in the story of Lazarus. The image of the Sacred Heart—in paintings, drawings, or statues—has been a source of consolation to Christians over the centuries as a reminder of Christ's willingness to suffer with and for us. This week, find an image of the Sacred Heart to meditate on and pray with. What do you see when you look at Jesus' sorrowing heart, pierced with thorns? Has your own heart ever felt this broken? What does Christ's empathy and love mean for you in your grieving?

The End of Grief

Begin by asking God to help you in your prayer and study. Then read through Revelation 21:1-6, a vision of the end of grief.

Revelation 21:1-6

¹Then I saw a new heaven and a new earth. The former heaven and the former earth had passed away, and the sea was no more. ²I also saw the holy city, a new Jerusalem, coming down out of heaven from God, prepared as a bride adorned for her husband. ³I heard a loud voice from the throne saying, "Behold, God's dwelling is with the human race. He will dwell with them and they will be his people and God himself will always be with them [as their God]. ⁴He will wipe every tear from their eyes, and there shall be no more death or mourning, wailing or pain, [for] the old order has passed away."

⁵The one who sat on the throne said, "Behold, I make all things new." Then he said, "Write these words down, for

they are trustworthy and true." ⁶He said to me, "They are accomplished. I [am] the Alpha and the Omega, the beginning and the end. To the thirsty I will give a gift from the spring of life-giving water."

After a few moments of quiet reflection on the passage, consider the information provided in Setting the Scene.

Setting the Scene

Once we have suffered the loss of someone we love, we wonder how to go on living. Does it help to know that Jesus grieved his beloved friend and grieves with us? Is it enough to remember that we are not alone in our grief and that the stories of companions like Ruth and Naomi point a way forward? Or do we long for more—the assurance that one day death and grief will be no more?

As Christians we also wonder about heaven as we mourn the death of a loved one. Will we ever see him or her again? What is heaven like? Where will we go when we die? Despite the fact that we evoke heaven twice whenever we pray the Our Father, we do not often hear about what the real hope of heaven might look or feel like. Heaven remains at best a mystery (and at worst a misunderstood cliché) in our collective imagination.

We read throughout the New Testament that Christ triumphed over death in the resurrection, so that we can now hope in eternal life. But we may not realize that heaven will bring the death of grief, too. Resurrection's promise means that eternal life with God will be free from sorrow and suffering. Revelation (the last book of the Bible) paints this comforting prospect in a dramatic vision of the new creation, heralded by angels and dazzling in splendor.

The author of Revelation, known as John, wrote in exile from the island of Patmos, where he exhorted first-century Christians to stand firm in the face of persecution (Rev 1:9). This book is a prime example of what is known as apocalyptic writing because it offers intense descriptions of the end times and the second coming of Christ that will usher in the new reign of God. Since Revelation is richly symbolic, it can be a daunting book to dive into for personal reflection. Yet its images and promises also explore in vivid language what awaits us in life beyond death. When we are yearning to know that the overwhelming intensity of grief will pass, Revelation offers hope that God will one day turn our tears into dancing.

The entire passage will be considered a few verses at a time. The questions in the margins are for discussion with others. If you are using these materials on your own, use the questions for personal reflection or as a guide to journaling.

Understanding the Scene Itself

¹Then I saw a new heaven and a new earth. The former heaven and the former earth had passed away, and the sea was no more. ²I also saw the holy city, a new Jerusalem, coming down out of heaven from God, prepared as a bride adorned for her husband.

At the end of the book of Revelation, the author John paints a vision of the new creation. The repetition of the word "new" throughout these verses emphasizes complete change and total renewal. The former heaven and earth are gone, and everything that exists now is unlike that which came before. This short passage contains both ending and beginning, the destruction of what was and the birth of what will be. John sees the "new Jerusalem" come down from God to meet earth, an image of a heavenly city where the faithful will live forever with God. Many of the Old Testament prophets offered similar visions: "See, I am creating new heavens / and a new earth; / The former things shall not be remembered / nor come to mind" (Isa 65:17). The idea of a perfect, physical city in which God's people will dwell has long given hope and comfort to those who suffer here on earth.

> Revelation invites us to consider eternity as a transformation of what already is.

This opening passage of chapter 21 describes a moment when heaven and earth meet—not that people go up to a distant heaven, but that a city prepared for them comes down to them where they are. This is a striking departure from many popular conceptions of heaven, and it invites us to reconsider our vision of eternity not as a departure elsewhere but as a transformation of what already is. This passage calls Christians to neither embrace nor reject our current earth—because it will eventually pass away—but to remember that a new earth will be part of God's new creation. The idea of heaven as a holy city suggests that there may be elements of eternal life that reflect or resemble what we have known here on earth, a comforting thought when we are longing to rejoin the ones we have lost.

What do you imagine heaven will be like?

John also compares the holy city to "a bride adorned for her husband" (v. 2). Marriage is a common symbol of God's covenant with the people throughout the Old Testament, but here we have the striking emphasis on the physical

beauty of both the bride and the holy city of the new creation. The prospect of eternal life brims with the joy, promise, and expectation of a wedding day, with every detail prepared and planned to create a perfect vision. The beauty and joy of this description stand in sharp contrast to our dark, colorless view of the world when we are grieving—which sets up our sorrowful hearts perfectly for the promise that comes in the verses that follow.

³I heard a loud voice from the throne saying, "Behold, God's dwelling is with the human race. He will dwell with them and they will be his people and God himself will always be with them [as their God]. ⁴He will wipe every tear from their eyes, and there shall be no more death or mourning, wailing or pain, [for] the old order has passed away."

No wonder these words are shouted from the throne, for they are a powerful declaration. We first hear Scripture's signal word to pay attention to something new that God is doing—"Behold." Then we are offered a remarkable promise: that God will dwell with humans forever, epitomizing God's name as Emmanuel ("God is with us" from Matt 1:23). Whereas the dwelling of God was once confined on earth to the temple or tabernacle, now the temple will be everywhere with God (Rev 21:22). As earlier in the passage, this image is the opposite of what we often imagine eternity to be like. Instead of people going up to heaven, God will come down to earth. As with the image of the new Jerusalem, the language of verses 3-4 draws from the prophetic tradition: "My dwelling shall be with them; I will be their God, and they will be my people" (Ezek 37:27). The proclamation also echoes Ruth's words to Naomi and God's promises to Israel that they will be God's people and God will be their God (Exod 6:7; Lev 26:12; Jer 30:22). God's identity and ours will remain defined by this relationship of abiding presence that will endure forever.

What does it mean for you that God promises to dwell forever with us?

Just as meaningful for us in our grief, God's enduring presence in the new creation means there will be no more tears, death, mourning, or pain. All these are *first* things of the *first* earth, sorrows and sufferings that will pass away. This promise of the end of grief itself is glimpsed in the Psalms ("You changed my mourning into dancing" [Ps 30:12]) and foretold in the prophets ("He will destroy death forever. / The Lord GOD will wipe away / the tears from all faces" [Isa 25:8]). Isaiah elaborates further upon the end of weeping in a powerful passage that foretells this passage in Revelation: "Instead, shout for joy and be glad forever / in what I am creating. / Indeed, I am creating Jerusalem to be a joy / and its people to be a delight; / I will rejoice in Jerusalem / and exult in my people. / No longer shall

Can you imagine life without weeping? What would replace your tears?

the sound of weeping be heard there, / or the sound of crying" (Isa 65:18-19). During times when tears seem to consume us, we can find solace in the prospect that crying will one day cease to exist. These verses promise us that grief is temporary, not lasting. Sorrow will be the first thing to be done away with in the new creation, destroyed even before sin (since sinners are dealt with later in verse 8).

⁵The one who sat on the throne said, "Behold, I make all things new." Then he said, "Write these words down, for they are trustworthy and true." ⁶He said to me, "They are accomplished. I [am] the Alpha and the Omega, the beginning and the end. To the thirsty I will give a gift from the spring of life-giving water."

The one on the throne is identified as Christ (see Rev 4), fulfilling Jesus' own words from the Gospel of Matthew: "in the new age, when the Son of Man is seated on his throne of glory" (Matt 19:28). Again in this passage we hear from Christ himself to "Behold"—the call to witness the new thing he is about to do. Now that sorrow and grief have been destroyed as the first signal of this new order of creation, the renewal of all things can begin. Christ commands John to write down what he hears and sees, and we are reassured to trust his words as witness and truth (v. 5).

What in your life today do you wish God would make new? Can you trust the hope of this transformation?

Three times in Revelation we find the title of Christ as Alpha and Omega (the first and last letters in the Greek alphabet), a perfect pairing

of beginning and end (1:8; 21:6; 22:13). The idea of Christ as the Word (John 1) takes on new meaning when we consider Christ to be the letters themselves, the elements that make up every word—and make his own words from the throne even more "trustworthy and true" (v. 5). This idea of God as beginning and ending encompasses all of history and time, catching up all our lives and experiences within its embrace. The invitation to consider a new image for God can be eye-opening and even refreshing in our grief. In particular, the title of Alpha and Omega allows us to hold two opposites together, a space of tension that often opens up in grief. For example, in this passage on the new creation as new beginning, Christ also announces that all things have been accomplished, echoing Jesus' last words on the cross: "It is finished" (John 19:30). Just as the former earth is being destroyed, Christ promises life-giving water for the thirsty. Especially as we mourn, this promise of eternal life can feel like a long drink of water after deepest thirst. All his actions here are Alpha and Omega: beginning in the midst of ending.

How has your image or understanding of God changed through grief?

Praying the Word / Sacred Reading

Return to the passage in Revelation 21:1-6, reading it carefully and prayerfully. Now imagine yourself into the scene as you ask God to open your heart to new perspectives on the story.

If you are using this study with a group, allow for time to read the full passage silently. Then you may wish to have one person read the reflection below while the others consider the questions quietly.

While we are grieving the death of a loved one, we often wish we could escape from the burden of grief, even for an hour. We long to have our old life back, where sadness did not define our days. We may even feel like the author of Revelation, exiled in punishment to a distant island, far from the friends and joy we once knew. But from his place of suffering and exile, John was given powerful visions of what eternal life would look like.

Close your eyes and imagine a new world without grief. Let yourself marvel at the prospect of seeing God in glory. Picture what it would be like to reunite with those you have lost, to share in the joy of their presence and never have to part again. What do you imagine this new heaven and earth might look, smell, sound, or feel like? What would you say to God? What would you say to your loved ones?

Let yourself bask in the hope of this promise. Like John, you can carry this vision with you, to let it shape your thoughts and strengthen your faith.

Living the Word

As we return from the apocalyptic images and words of Revelation to our everyday lives, we may take heart in Paul's words from the letter to the Romans: "I consider that the sufferings of this present time are as nothing compared with the glory to be revealed for us" (Rom 8:18). As you pray to carry the vision of eternal glory into your present grief, notice if your images or understanding of God start to shift too.

Grief can ultimately transform our relationship with God as we experience God's presence, comfort, or calling in new ways in this changed chapter of life. God may be comforter, listener, mourner, companion, or source of hope. No matter how we experience God in grief, Scripture reminds us that God remains with us in the pit of suffering, at the tomb, and on the last day. The word "behold" can echo in our prayer as we continue to work through our grief in the light of our faith, hoping that God is still at work in our lives doing something new.